Life in B minor

Michele Lalla

Translated from Italian by the author

English version edited by
William Bromwich

Cover: Caterpillars (author)

First edition: March 2021

Epigraph

*At times everything is there from the beginning
whereas at other times nothing is there,
the beginning is the obstacle, and
a terrible enlightenment is born.*

*An open mind enables us to come into contact
with something before it falls into oblivion
as a result of indifference or indolence.*

Table of contents

Caterpillar words

Words that speak of pain
may lead us to
thoughts of hope and love
but we need to go beyond the self,
beyond the mythical Ulysses,
the self-centered heartless hero
who cast loyalty to the wind.

What if everything we need to know
is already written?

Writing literature
is an almost impossible task
but I cannot bear the thought of surrender,
and try to draw words out from cocoons,
mixed with lapis-lazuli geometries
bringing together dense intersections,
of links between sense and nonsense.

We have to go beyond advertising
the aims of writing, not as a pastime,
but as way to bear witness
(not militant sentiment)
inspired by the books we have devoured,
not by the poetry of the moment.

Daily routines

Circadian rhythms contaminate us.

Morning: I look at myself in the mirror
              and the sky is like water.

Afternoon: I delude myself in the mirage.

Evening: Fireflies light up my eyes.

As a caterpillar I set off on the journey
through the land of dreams and the self
marking out my territory to make myself known
to any available females, like all males,
sending out a warning to others:
"Woe to the intruder".

For us it is a question of reproduction,
for you it is a symptom of obsession:
myopia and dullness, racist sentiment and fear.

Self-centeredness

Fear makes even the shadows afraid
giving rise to senseless anguish.
Many of us blame foreigners, leading to
thoughts about development and backwardness.

People need to feel a sense of well-being
and are committed to progress from willpower:
"If I am well, the whole world will be well,"
they say to make sense of their lives
unaware that hope fades fast.

People may not hold in with paying taxes,
but join together and march against the State
which they consider to be a hostile force.
They then complain about it not being there
in the case of need when things go wrong.

Grub-employees

The State leaves the weak to their own devices
while supporting the strongest
and everyone thinks only of himself.
Some live in a land of milk and honey
not caring about the rest.
Others who are in trouble protest in the streets,
demanding jobs, but once hired,
they lose the will to change things.
They spend their earnings
when they can but are not prepared
to help the State, that is absent without leave.
Maybe we are all absentees,
devouring the goods that belong to everybody,
and eating to excess,
like scoundrels trying to lead the good life
but bereft of values.

Pleasure-loving

Many people enjoy the good life,
and are obsessed like fools about three things:
money, sex and fun.
What about the rest? They don't care.
You see: think creatively.

Many people complain but fail to make an effort
when things go wrong.
It is all the fault of others, or the government,
a band of thieves.

Many people make sacrifices but fail to reach
their goals, while grifters drain off
the money of others but come out clean.

Many say the yoke weighs heavily on the poor
and not on the wealthy
but the poor have often approved of it all
like a mass of displaced caterpillars.

Many people are good, and most are satisfied
with their income because if they are careful
how they spend it, they make it to the end
of the month and can tell everyone to go to hell.

Country of dispatch

The place they send us to may be the worst.
Everybody harbors their own illusions
pretending to ignore the fact that
we all may end up in the bad place.

Many people think they are clever
even when they are up to their necks
damaging the environment without a thought
in spite of the warning signs.
Maybe only the great flood will bring us down
from the throne of arrogance.

Caterpillars know what the place is
because that is where they live their lives
heeding the warning:
"Wake up when you hear the alarm going off."

Morning awakenings

The alarm clock goes off:
you wake with a gentle yawn
your face dazzles me
your body welcomes me
on my awakening.

My heart beats faster and faster
as we come together
lost in a loving embrace
my soul vanishing
almost as if in pain.

"A grub has no conscience,"
they say. And so I hang on
in a state of inertia,
struggling against faces
and pointless quarrels
while listening to voices
in the morning light.

Voices and visions

Voices in the morning
as the blackbirds sing.
You are close to me,
with your divine mouth.

We exchange glances
but you remain detached
and the wait continues.

Your warmth
hits me like a storm of kisses
bringing forth joy
as the rain catches us lying on the grass.

The evening comes
with you and you join
with me in a whirlwind of feelings.

We kiss in our sleep
and drift into a dream
with love all around.

The evil of all

The dream of love hurts me.

Don't tell me that the evil of a worm
doesn't exist, although I resist unarmed.
Walk across my barren land,
and feel the pain it entails.

Come with me as I take you
down a grassy path
to our secret garden.

Look down where you see no light
on the ground under your feet
and you will find the thread to stitch
our painful wounds.

I lead you down to the vineyard,
pouring out poetry like sweet wine
to give you pleasure.

We savor the scent of
fermenting grapes
in wicker baskets,
exchanging glances.

Do without hope

In a basket of fresh looks, *there*,
you place heaven beyond this *here*.

Heaven is our existence lived here.
You only see it if you look from there,
from heaven, the point of view of love,
changing the perspective on pain.

Here everyone bears their cross
and swears to heaven raising their own voice,
either angry or resigned. Over there
we find hope but it is over here
that our freedom begins
enabling us to find blessings
without being overcome by anxiety.

There is no this here *or* that there,
but only here *and* there.

Faces of being

Human beings are the center of the universe
with the God in which they immerse themselves.

The god of a caterpillar is no different
from a God made in your image
because that God reflects many faces,
good and ugly, but all of them in harmony.
Even the caterpillar has its place
taking on the semblance of the universe.

You cannot see how I see.

Leave me in the shadows as the light floods in
with a wave of hormones
unleashing impulses.
In the dark I see illusions leading to nothing:
only then will I exist and find peace
at the bottom of my heart.

Charity

Some dare to say:
"It is time for charity."
Maybe for some this means
the time of awakening,
but charity makes you a human being
every time, and every time is the right time.

Charity has always been hard for us
as we all look out for ourselves,
and fight tooth and nail to get ahead.

It is the same for all of you, but there are people
who make donations to help those who suffer.
Some who are unable to go on just give in
and find a way to put an end to it
rather than living like a bandit.

We find a way to show solidarity
when the State fails to do so:
no-one contributes as a way to replace the State.

Evading taxes

Some refuse to cooperate with the State,
they burn their tax returns in the streets
and act like bandits, expressing their contempt
for public services, and failing to take care
of public property.
They take bribes whenever they can
and look for ways to avoid paying
their fair share,
while filling their pockets and stomachs.

These individuals urge the depleted State
to defend and educate the citizens,
and to help those in need.
If they are the ones in need,
but really unworthy, don't worry:
we caterpillars are alien to such ideas and warn
that black cinders will fall from the sky.

The attack

Flocks of birds soar overhead
as dark clouds gather.

Starlings swirl around
threatening the grub
who is unaware of the impending attack,
that is totally unforeseen.

The caterpillar seeks shelter
from the ambush above
but the blackbird swoops in from the side.
He feels the sharp pain of the peck
when it is too late and he succumbs,
the victim of the fatal attack.

What you have

When accused of devastating the Earth
we caterpillars smile through gritted teeth
because men don't see what they are doing
destroying the environment.
The destruction of nature
is passed down from father to son
due to madness or corrupt instincts.

The caterpillar strips florid branches
off the mulberry tree
while humans devastate the earth with fire,
poison the water with acid, and
pollute the air with smog and greenhouse gases.
But what of the oceans, the Amazon, the Arctic?
There is no escaping the urges
that corrupt the human heart with wars
arising from basic needs:
food, clothing, and sex.

Real or virtual needs undermine the intellect.
You are what you are because you have what
you have, but also because you don't have
what you do not have.
There is no way to escape
comings and goings.

Blessed first

In the comings and goings
of the breathless crowds
we are the ones who aren't blessed:
"I crush you like a worm,"
"You disgust me because you are a worm."
These are the insults of depraved men,
wandering round like desperate souls
or beings without a soul.

Human beings alienated from the world
have created a God in the sky
who placed the elected ones in heaven
and the others in hell. For caterpillars
a God in the sky means nothing:
we may as well turn our antennae on Him.

Everyone competes to be the first
while the others wait in line,
gnashing their teeth.
We are part of a circle:
we are neither the first nor the last
only the beating of the heart
living out its allotted time in a temple.

The first catch-all

The state is always the same:
a group enjoying its privileges
obsessed with self-preservation,
rather than with improving society,
as everyone enjoys their own advantages.
The opposition makes a challenge
and raises protests in a bid
to reduce politics to emotions:
"No more corruption.
Vote now and the winner takes all.
We will govern only if we have 100 per cent."

The leaders made "honesty" their slogan,
the disgruntled voters really believed them
and voted for them: their newspaper put forward
policies based only on appearances,
with deals made under-the-counter.

The voters feel more and more fatigue,
not knowing who to turn to.

Omitted variables

Many use old instead of new items
because the new soon becomes the old
and used items are seen as something to cast off.

Gross domestic product is like silk
enriching us in the same way as an egg,
but we need a mulberry tree,
as the more we consume,
the more we need to produce.

Many reasonings
leave out a number of variables,
focusing on only two or three
but leaving everything else unchanged:
with the environment treated as a mulberry tree,
the woods, orchards and crops disappear.

This also applies to certain economists:
if you leave the euro you can devalue,
the more goods you export,
the more you can spend.

The reactions of others are ignored,
but beatings will soon be upon us,
to the detriment of the most vulnerable.

Uncertainty

Even if the mists over the harbor lift at dawn,
that doesn't settle the matter of where to land,
and the wait goes on
amid the heaving waves.

You are alone in every decision
when the umbilical cord is cut
with the wind in the sails
leading towards the spider's web.

Those who don't take risks give their advice,
while those who throw the dice
glare into the fire with the shadows
playing tricks on our eyes.

Meanwhile the spider weaves a silky web
of rules and regulations imposed from above.

Clichés

The country is supposed to be where people
are close to each other with no borders,
where collective memory brings back to life
so many timeless stories.

Freedom remains outside the frame
and needs a different humus.
Proximity is like a cactus of conformism
fastening you with bonds
that are harmful if they are too close.
You don't leave in a fit of madness
but to find a place,
sometimes failing and coming back.

You never go back to the starting point
but go forward in order to be behind,
setting your conscience aside
pulling the strings in the dark
of puppets at the center of things.
Yes, men and caterpillars resemble each other.

The essential act

Man is no more than a caterpillar
in semblance, while acting like the almighty,
he destroys the environment and living beings
but not for the purposes of survival.

Man created God in his image and likeness,
and a kingdom where he will be bored to death.
Man fights tooth and nail,
ignoring the wind and the waves.
He strives for personal profit with malice
even if this leaves behind a wasteland,
while desisting is the essential act
abandoning yourself to love
against all existential dilemmas
to rediscover a passionate heart.

Democracy

Many people have a passion
but only for football and their home town.
It is often the case that people quarrel
over politics but only if it is to their advantage,
for a free lunch, a job, or a promise.

Many people are good as long as everyone else
keeps quiet or stays home, and there are people
generous enough
to open their heart to the world,
but the needs of others bore them.
"Who cares?" they shrug.

Some people stand up and say:
You kill democracy if you can't eat.
They may die as they wish but we need to
entrust our well-being to noble leaders
and not to the madding crowd.

Democracy is the common good
to nurture in our hearts and minds
while keeping our leaders in check
but for most people the good life
means doing as they wish until the end.

What remains, after breaking the banks?

Poison

When the barriers to chaos break down,
then poison seeps into the system
and this is worse than the stain
on the heart or the eyes that are
fearful, distrustful or arrogant.

Without a code of ethics
and honest independent journalists,
the media manipulates public opinion
with a cascade of disinformation
acquiring power without responsibility
and a policy that is far-sighted.

People demand easy solutions
that are not a burden on them,
but populists give them a thrashing.

Educating the mind

Populists give voters a thrashing,
using "honesty" as a slogan
and telling indigestible lies,
but previously they neglected them
or flattered them with false promises,
stoking up fury and anger.

Voters are at the mercy of the media
electing those who promise
the past in the future,
dashing their hopes with conjecture.
Those who are not patient with their opponents
make them become impatient.
Those who are not capable of critical reasoning
take up the hatchet and go on the warpath.
Those who don't know
how to mediate in conflict
risk ending up in a state of paralysis
or fighting outside forces.

Intolerance of all things foreign
closes the mind. People must be
educated to broaden their vision,
with the wisdom of the heart, while
recognizing the good and evil within.

Emotional fidelity

Good and evil depend on our aims
and values, but what do people do?
They act as the enemies of freedom,
while taking care of their interests
and relying on fidelity based on emotion.
But fate will partly be determined
by those who are elected to help the voters.

Our leaders forget their promises:
they often fail to perform their duties,
but use propaganda to gain advantages
for their cronies, making a fool of voters
with reforms that leave unchanged
the state cloaked with art and malice.

Forbidden fruit

Malice cloaks our misdeeds,
so everyone engages in it:
promises are not honored
with pensions and income seen as a right.

Where do they get the money
to pay for what they have promised?
They don't raise money by taxing the rich
according to their incomes
but cut back on health spending,
and the judicious are aware
that the sick will be denied care.
The provinces are abolished
resulting in unsafe roads.

Politics is a complicated business:
politicians talk about the Garden of Eden,
telling the citizens not to eat the forbidden fruit:
"Don't eat imported truth".
Meanwhile, the butterflies in power
enjoy the forbidden fruit aware of
the good and evil inside us.

Saints alive

Good and evil are to be found in our hearts.
Grubs harbor them in their bellies,
where the saints fused them together
with the name of love in an incongruous union.
If we pull them apart, we call God into question.

Holiness no longer gives rise to the need
to display it as the virtue that it is.
Religion is no more:
those in power consecrate themselves
and popes and prelates do so unashamedly.

If there is an afterlife, surprises will abound:
caterpillars will shine unexpectedly on high
in the divine light
while due to the havoc they have wreaked
humans will beg for forgiveness
in a ditch.

All in the light

The last one into the grave may be the first,
dancing in circles where there is no order.
In the after-life everyone is praised
by all those present.
No-one is excluded
but all are happy together in the light.
Victims and perpetrators tend to receive
the same amount of praise,
and harm appears to be a gift.

We may not know, but if there is a God,
He grants forgiveness
as the Almighty
loves all living beings.
Our desire for eternity
leads us to a sense of abandonment,
while our thirst for possessions
results in a sense of loss.
The omnipotent self seeks the suppression
of evil, imploding all that is good.

History returns

They say one thing and do another:
those with fascist tendencies are in our midst.
You can tell them from their footsteps
and the stench of the clothes they never cast off,
their attraction to places worse than sewers
their tendency to violence,
the blank expression on their faces,
and their slave-like devotion to the leader.

With shaven heads, longing for the past,
they harangue those who are foreigners
with no thought for other people.
Caterpillars seek to close their borders
to new arrivals
defending their backyard, tooth and nail,
but whereas caterpillars struggle to survive
donkeys roam menacingly around
in the gathering storm.

Self-destruction

Human beings have fought their way
to the top of the food chain,
but due to their short-sightedness
may destroy themselves and all living beings.
While caterpillars are subject to the law,
humans claim to be exempt,
bewailing the harm
they have done to themselves and
the world they have ravaged.

Human beings think they are smart
but are dazzled by the greed for profit.
They survive by denying the fact that
the environment is exploited
without restraint and devastated
by cataclysms that risk annihilating us.
Our existence is an unstable mix
of good and evil
reliant on freedom.

Good and evil

They say that misfortune is having
good and evil in every being:
the caterpillar is no exception,
and may even be the most intriguing.

Human beings represent the fusion
of two opposites,
making them admirable creatures.
In the case of a fall this means redemption,
in certainty it makes us fallible,
in pride it instils humility,
in the chaos of love,
it gives us a stimulus
to seek closure.

Good and evil need simply
to come together as one:
their fusion is also in God
who is whole.

Detail

There can be no unity without community,
that takes a lifetime to build,
with painstaking attention to detail,
but a moment to destroy.

Detail casts light on the divine,
though some say the devil is in the detail.
In the darkness we look for a glimmer of hope
searching for the female caterpillar.

All is lost in trivial matters,
reflecting our identity.
Other people appear to be foreign to us,
and wrongly we want them to be extradited.
Good thoughts come from an awareness
that contamination can enrich our lives.

Metamorphosis

Cross-cultural contamination
can serve a useful purpose
if we bind the strands together
enabling us to look with fresh eyes.

Our lives materialize
as if in a kaleidoscope of dragonflies
entangled with pistils
swooping down in flight
gnawing through strings
looking beyond the horizon of cravings
detached from chaos and pride.

The caterpillar is left all alone.

Metamorphosis takes place
between verse and phalli [1]
with words going beyond practice,
while the caterpillar is under the illusion
that he is a butterfly.

Mirrors and illusions

Some people are deluded, convinced that
they are alive although they can no longer see.
They get tangled up with presumption
changing the vision of the silkworm
while contemplating different stages of life,
watching their wings flutter past
the larva devoured by indignity.

Time turns the caterpillar into a pupa,
then into a chrysalis,
the cradle of past troubles or
the crystal of a mock death,
then it is no longer a silkworm:
metamorphosis at the birth of the cocoon
is something like a wedding.

Contaminations of texts

Metamorphosis transforms the first draft [2]
bringing the cocoon back to life
even when the plot grinds to a halt,
leaving us lifeless and detached.
The past is placed in the trash [3]
ending up in intensive care.

A whole new verse takes shape,
an excerpt from a book, an imitation,
falling into place out of desperation,
pouring blood-red ink into bloodless
words in flight like a butterfly
on the way to the library seeking
dreams, cycles, and seasons.
In a perpetual circular motion,
the woodworm gnaws its way
through the wood,
devouring the paper of learning,
on his journey towards cleverness.

Pro-creation

The journey into ingenuity does not reduce
the butterfly's determination to go back to
the mask of the caterpillar no longer living.
The butterfly closes its wings in the shadows
while the maggot revenant flies towards chaos,
masking the divine right,
with humans no longer distinct from God.

The caterpillar that fails to reproduce will die:
to perpetuate himself he needs
to lay eggs after devouring books.
He finds his origin in the mold,
a mulch of syllables and paper,
with an uncertain outcome.
After swallowing it all,
he takes on a new shape
and returns to intensive care.

Truth and chance

The shape stands out in a circle of stars:
from the egg to the caterpillar to the butterfly
to the chrysalis to the egg,
the circle of life is complete.

You die to live and live to die,
lingering on the bookshelves
in stories handed down in books
in the circle of life embracing myths.

In the beginning there was chaos, and the chaos
was sorted into words, and the words
of each one of us put together stories
at times adhering to truth
reflecting simple reality:
tales and stories turning on chance,
fading away with the futility of time.

Labyrinths of stories

Time is governed by laws
in which stories appear as invisible wrecks
overflowing with visible characters
displaying chaotic traits
influencing chance.
Stories form a labyrinth of vice
depriving you of the chance
to go back to the origins,
forcing you to move forward.

Only then can you head towards the mirage
awakening from a slumber of magic tales
amazed by secret thoughts,
while embarking on an arduous journey.

The joy of rhymes

Words that bring ideas to life
are the fertile ground we use to plant cuttings
on a journey to the heart of the matter
using maps with contrasting colors.

We struggle in our sleep
but overcome it with rhymes
on ill-fated journeys,
constructing out of chaos
pathways that go beyond familiar tropes:
journeys from/into the stories we devour.

Macchiaiola memory

Setting off on a journey in your head
means tracing ghosts in naivety,
following in the footsteps of
Ulysses, the treacherous hero.

You may lose your nerve and become neurotic,
turning into a caterpillar devouring books
to feed on knowledge of spiritual mysteries.
The kaleidoscope glistens with
arabesques of verse
viewed through lenses
refracting on crystals
each time along different lines.

After reading many books
you recall only excerpts or scraps:
only fragments survive,
images of life imprinted on the skin.

Inebriation and verses

Your hungry lips sip the wine
from the chalice of ecstasy,
with glimpses of life,
flashes of enthusiasm,
and euphoric phrases
flowing through your heart,
under the sun in a dream of love.

Your lips brush up against the chalice
reflecting greed,
avoiding the traces of alcohol,
flowing over into a dream
that uncovers your breasts with kisses,
while the eyelashes of vampire-sleep
shine in the worm's dream of virtue.

Pointless questions

Dreams: stories vanishing at the break of day.
Removal: ghosts coming back without delay.
Existence: enigmas of various states of chaos.

The caterpillar dreams and wriggles
on the mulberry tree
but writing interrupts
the stream of weak thought
following in our footsteps
towards unknown links
seeking to answer so many questions:
Where will man be?
What do I, a humble caterpillar, know
of the man who makes himself God?
You, God, where do you exist?
In a chalice of sweet wine?

Being and Nothingness
flow along with the wine,
drifting in the breeze,
floating in the water,
between sips of wine
while the caterpillar is overwhelmed
in a sea of bookish learning.

Comparative deities

From tomes of spiritual mysteries
to Barbera, fleshy lips
brush against the chalice of wine
envisioning salvation
in the euphoria of inebriation.

God has a plan for man,
but the god of the caterpillar is no less than
the God of man that dominates the universe.
If you turn away from blasphemy
you shall sip the wine that leads to the Lord.

Here you have religious scriptures
consisting of tomes of holy writings
clashing with logic.

There you have the religion of the caterpillar,
stirring like a dragon
facing the onslaught of the web of sin.

Forced to live

The mirage of the spider comes into view
like a death threat for the caterpillar
slithering along the path,
gazing into depths of the abyss
inching forward with fractal steps
into a sea of long-distance journeys,
floundering among the broken spears
of water on the rocks of hunger.

The setting sun drops down behind the sails
that glide along while fishing for apples
from the tree of the knowledge of good and evil.
A cry goes up from the sails:
You need to go beyond Nothingness.

Like a caterpillar the state is ready
to contemplate the catharsis
that melts the Adam's apple away.

The pain of waiting

Treachery lurks on the rock:
a voice quakes like an illusion
between the blue desert and the ozone.

The sunny afternoon is like a catalysis
in which in a state of paralysis
you fade like a mirage.

The waves drench you with reality
while waiting for a voice that will not speak,
and a gust of wind in the sail
that will allow you to drift away.

The pain of waiting will not be in vain:
in the end you welcome a grub
like a gardenia floating on a cloud
penetrating you with a piercing glance.

Little ones

If you look without being short-sighted,
you will discover beyond appearances
that it takes little for the exultation
of a little one.

If you look and lower your guard,
you will discover in your heart
that it doesn't take much to light up the face
of a little one.

Whether you succeed or fail
may be due to ignorance or laziness,
but it takes little for the serenity
of a little one.

It takes little to put wings
on your head and take flight
but it takes an effort to break down
the barriers that make it impossible
to defeat slavery in the guise
of freedom that is only apparent.

Fragile vision

Freedom refracts on the mirror,
casting light on opposite paths and
revealing a fragility that confuses
right and wrong.
Those who are false take a step forward,
provoking a response.

Dismayed by change,
we feel pain in the shadow of evil,
and anger at the sharp claws of the ones who
crush the hands of the innocent and powerless,
yesterday, today and tomorrow.

We live in anguish about right and wrong,
true and false, but if we give in to despair
we are no better than larvae or the sons of Cain.

Outcast fiber

We have no reason to give in to despair,
say those at the top of the food chain.

Those who are absent are ill-treated,
and caterpillars are like monsters.

With the survival of the fittest,
caterpillars are trampled underfoot.

The world governed by the eternal myth
of Ulysses the imposter is not the only one,
with a bloodthirsty monster
sailing across the high seas:
there is also the world of the caterpillar
following the dictates of the heart
and demonstrating his love
for the religion of the world he lives in.
He intended to devote his life on earth
to the faith of Buddha and Christ
but clearly lacked the temperament.

Digesting volumes

All that exists is natural,
even if it wrong: if it is, let it be,
if it is not, let it not be, and amen.

I may be a caterpillar and not a dolmen:
I may even be the wise man of tomorrow
as I have devoured the Treccani: [4]
it appears strange, but it is natural
to become shriveled
like a blade of grass on the ground
at the corner of the street.

Growing up in a library
I acquired learning
among the volumes and tomes
ending up with an indigestion of waste paper,
but then I evacuated them
on the face of the learned.

Unknown city

Worm-eaten volumes constitute
an unnatural setting
for an abstract understanding
of what remains of the city
as we blink into the headlights.

The headlights peek out from behind the cloud
amid the lies [5] of the firefly on rundown streets.
This is the city you do not know
with its commodification of goods and bodies.

The headlights peek out from the gloomy cloud
as a crowd of pale faces offer to labor
for a pittance at the gates of smog:
men driven by the need to work.

The headlights peek out in the magical light
as the crowds tune in to techno-music.
Some start fighting with the dead,
wallowing in the pursuit of pleasure.

Vanity of the rite

We have set certain days aside
to remember misdeeds
with prayers that leave them intact,
but for caterpillars, hypocrisy is never an option.

Words for describing misconduct
are full of sound and fury:
nobody knows how to prevent wars
in which the flesh and the earth burn.

The cry goes up:
"Stand up if you are down on your knees",
but impotence masks the pain
hiding reality from our eyes.

Acquiescence makes our hearts go to sleep:
and stamping our feet in protest is not enough,
if we are downtrodden again.

The need for food

Only immediate needs count in the mind
of the hungry caterpillar
who is fasting on the honey of dreams,
stirring him from his slumbers
but making him faint
as he wakes up to the fraud.

I gobble up fragments of text
and complain that pulses are for caterpillars
while paper is only fit for woodworm
and all flesh is grass
as time marches relentlessly on.

I force myself not to give up the battle
with the basket woven from words
shaping vanishing consciences
and unimagined ghosts:
wax-like figures burned at the stake.

In/vocation

Don't mold the wax figures anymore:
the shadows of ghosts tear them apart
as the raging blaze spreads out.

Don't patch up the caterpillar
as his heart will become fainter
if the borderless darkness awaits him.

Paint the forgotten effigy and don't give up:
share the treasures you have accumulated,
and hope beyond your immediate confines.

Powerless in the face of wrongdoing
I refuse to give up.
In the name of truth
I defend you,
for the sake of freedom
I extend the hand of friendship to you.

Ominous signs

At the stroke of a hand
the heart is thrown away
to be fed to the dogs,
the wineskins are drained,
the flesh dried out.

The caterpillar preens himself
like a knight in shining armor,
powerful men are envied,
bullies imitated,
humble men cast aside.

Myths, sophistry, and rumors
fill the vain and vacuous minds of lost souls.

Defeat is carved in stone
on a sign at the entrance.

Daily thorns

Defeat starts from the prism
distorting our vision of the world
and the cactus that comes from Nature.

Every day we stitch up our wounds,
then wield a razor to reopen them.

Every day the earth is covered
with nettles and cobwebs.

Every day Nothingness attacks the mind
and loneliness drives out sympathy.

Every day love turns into sickness
if we fail to curb the spread of selfishness.

Every day we can uphold the humanity
(or the caterpillar) as long as we learn humility
and persist in cultivating virtue.

Virtue and vice

The caterpillar has no virtues, only vices,
as it is unclean and despicable,
an abominable putrid maggot,
unworthy of distinction:
grubs, woodworm, aphids, moths
worming their way through books,
with weevils, teredos, snout-beetles and worms,
slobbery, filthy, disgusting garbage,
an effigy of slime that destroys
the purity of functions, a blend
of expanding thoughts of mud,
the simulacrum of a dragon
ashamed to express passion.

Union of opposites

Harsh words are needed to respond to
the annoying complaints
of caterpillars in striped stockings,
as annoying voices lead us backwards.

Only conflict can ever break our chains.

During a revolt we don't deface images
portraying identities, effigies or souls.

The union of opposites is under attack:
meeting places are under pressure
reducing them to narrow confines.

Moving the castle makes the union fall apart:
we need to debunk certain lies
and defend the union of opposites
that is coming under fire
in the shadows. [6]

Dreams of zeroes

Even the meanest of caterpillars aspires to
fresh air, space and a breath of life,
though not to the nectar of the gods.

Even sinister caterpillars facing doom
have the right to grazing or *uria* [7]
and to fly as high as a kite in the orchard.

Even zeroes like us yearn for contact
with the female of the species
brushing on the pollen of antlers
or biting on flesh
rather than being worthless crawling beings
afraid of being pecked to death by poultry
or being *sticchio* [8] of slobber and slime,
larvae without blood and fire
(the wood of others at the stake burns better).

Presumed lootings

The fire in my belly burns
to digest volumes of knowledge.
It is an arduous task to rediscover
the fire of my being
but always better than
the fire of others.

                              Maybe it is pride
that strikes idiots like a wooden mallet
but the fire is mine and I keep it as it is:
for better or worse, it is the fire of the Self.

I have learned encyclopedias by heart
and mashed up [9] countless theories:
losing my way among metaphors e metonyms
I have pillaged everything.
                                In a few words
this is an essay unworthy of mimesis.

Blaze of reaction

Leave the fire alone, as it burns
not as a grub. When you are a butterfly:
once the heart is turned it lights up like a flame
in your eyes, and I see only concern
for the other sex even if she is only a stigma.

We can't resist the blaze of hunger
in the fire burning the woods:
it has the heat of life
and the coldness of death,
so I follow the instinct that leads me to
the fire of hell and takes me away.

The flame is an elusive element
quickening alchemies and slowing compounds
with ambiguities casting light on opposites.

Immutable repetition

Ambiguity is to be found in the word
that fails to reveal my countenance
or my habit of consuming or rather
devouring books in pursuit of my dreams.

Visions turn into experience,
reality changes in appearance.
'All the same' does not help you to vote,
but the choice of the least-worst in public life
serves to avoid the worst.
                              See how I struggle:
tell me I am indifferent to politics,
and that I reflect only on how I am changing.

It is not only my skin that changes appearance,
in some places, silky, in others, rough:
wings transport me to a place of beauty
in flights of ecstasy ascending to the gates.

Digesting legacies

In the heat sharp stones press our bodies
up against the prickly pears
like a thorn in the flesh,
and spasms of hunger
prick our tongues
longing for figs.

During the downturn we will have no figs:
recriminating us for not voting wisely
will not help to avoid the worst.
If we fail to make our minds up in time
we have no way of knowing
if we have a second chance
but there will be less to eat.

Indigestible meals satiate
our pangs of hunger
like shards of pottery.
Facing uncertainty
leads to flights of fantasy
amid the omens of the future
with neither wings
nor ways of understanding.

Onomatopoeia

I do not have the insight of a prophet,
but a medley [10] of thoughts turned over [11]
by wishes *sbrigola* [12] in the eye:
a caterpillar sailor following
the routes and making his way at the helm,
where the wind blows [13] ruffled. [14]
It grapples [15] and carries [16] the sails forward,
it gets excited [17] at the touch of the *ruga*, [18]
truffles or Tortuga,
but the part of me that is stupid [19] tortures me
and the cockade [20] causes me [21] to make
illiterate grimaces [22] at *ciamboni* [23]
that you believe to be cannon.

Maybe we are soft caterpillars
and *trumpdicks*, [24]
all spineless [25]
between veiled grasp-robbery, [26]
castellans gathering [27] *lovrogance* [28]
in the aquarium of the galley attempting
to overcome the hammering waves.

Un/bridle blocks

In the torpedo the wave hammer beats the timer
and the sail of the water chamber
swells beyond the flow of years
with the pendulous weight of a pipe
vibrating at the swing of the pointer [29]
moving forward and unleashing chaos.
Those in power who easily fool us
are good at taking care of their own interests.

From the center of the iris
with the ray percussion-pins of a laser
the skipper aims the torpedo at the target
while peering into the dark.

When the target is finally struck
we end up in the air, in the water,
then in the resuscitation chamber.

Those who insist on destruction will end up
in the same place but unable to stand the heat.

Hypocrisy of the short-sighted

The driving force of history is fear
but can a caterpillar be brave?
A sniveling mucus full of dregs, filthy rubbish,
dirty obscene awkward *ruffa*,[30]
ugly disgraceful grotesque foulness,
disfigured monstrous degenerate beak,
a filthy despicable worm.

Ridiculous and impossible feelings
are hidden in the caterpillar's soul,
but his understanding is no worse
than that of men, who often understand
only when it is too late.
Then they shed hypocritical tears,
and the stubborn ones
are framed by the camera lens
with their limited vision,
admirable icons devoid of meaning.

Literary freedom

The caterpillar is not an icon on the sails,
but the rottenness of the mast, which crafts
its destiny of being in nature and fails:
a breath of dust in the wind and drafts.

Words of fiction burn there,
an effigy of repressed freedom,
here on the shrouds there is liberation
from a tangle of foolish ideas,
inflated by letters without science,
pleased with a vague exact sense,
as intuition does not yield to the facts
and resists foolish ambitions.

I write freely about misdeeds,
without a great deal of learning:
a degree of ignorance may be more genuine
than too much culture at gut level.

Deepest wishes

Knowledge can instill consciousness
of the self and a world of insight
but where restlessness has a presence,
bewilderment can sow doubt in the mind:
devouring so many volumes
has taken its toll on my digestion.

Tired and disillusioned I strive for peace
and not tiger-faced battles,
which I fought tooth and nail
among the followers of Ulysses the amoral,
causing so much damage to those
who believed in a false truce.

I wish for peace energetically and am deluded,
as nothing more in the heart is quiet
in the hour of martyrdom and at Easter.
Peace becomes at Christmas,
that is where I shall lie in my grave,
in a perfect shroud of snow.

Christmas peace

The air is quilted with bows and pins,
flitting to and fro or lighting up with snow
as the bell tower rings out with a peal
of Christmas bells giving shape
to every shadow.

Some say a miracle will take place
rooting out hypocrisy, unmasking impostors,
purging greed, responding to our ancestral fears.

Many have come to heed the call
but I'm not sure whether to come or go.

I stand waiting, flecked with snow,
for a voice to overcome my resistance.
Only those who seek peace
will find their hidden voice:
"Come brother, I give you my peace".

Open doors

Ritual voices say "Peace be with you"
at Christmas as they are among friends,
though their fortunes are not the same:
  Do not close the doors!

Peace is broken down by resentment,
and unity is destroyed by distrust,
blocking the way towards communion:
  Do not lock the doors!

Let us lift the holy chalice up together
to drive back the scary ghosts
lowering the mask of the scepter,
separated by state borders:
  so that it is not a farce.
Let us close the gap between humans,
to shake off false images
  and open our doors!

Robbery

Alerted by the whistling of a starling
the goshawk dives down,
draws out its claws, and flies back:
a robbery dictated by hunger.

The man, hearing the clucking of the partridge,
aims, shoots and kills:
a robbery for the sake of sport.

Other robberies are the result of neglect:
the oceans covered in algae and tar,
the earth contaminated by waste,
forest fires lit by speculators.

Like the Charge of the Light Brigade
when the time comes
we will live or die,
breathing in layers of smog
hanging on a precarious thread.

Masters of the Universe

Precariousness does not figure in the mind
of the Masters of the Universe who ignore
the abyss at their feet and put on a display
of arrogance under many pretexts
with a strong apparatus around them
to preserve their domination.

Only the naïve tear down the curtain.
    Who are they really? They are
the Masters of Exploitation,
the Masters of Power,
the Masters of Money,
the Masters of War,
who arm men made of clay,
Samson's emulators and followers.

The naïve ones still hope at a distance
placing their faith in ethics, which is human,
shouting: "UNITED WE STAND"
to dispel fears and illusions.

Cain's Kingdom

A cry goes up among the plumes of smoke,
amid the struggles for land
with spiders weaving tangled webs
and thrushes preying on cicadas.

The hunger for land makes us take up arms
as massacres take place among the rushes:
history has moved on from the time
that imposed inevitable pathways.

Among the burnt rushes, with no more thrushes
or cicadas, the cobwebs are now empty:
the hand of Cain reigns over all.

The need for space blinds us,
bringing down a frost among fraternal souls,
with nothing left for grubs and men.

Dis/appearance

If there is Nothing, the grub goes for it [31]
as it is the opposite of Eternity,
consoling the grub and making sense
of the whole in spite of its futility.
And so the *sluggutting* [32] *mussels* [33] itself
and with morsels [34] *borborumbles* [35] virtue
of *musicfarts* [36] dictated to mussels and glue
of hypertext struggling against vogue, fashion,
square for the *breloque,* [37] which is an illusion,
people *servazza* [38] *lentonguing* [39] net
friends, *crutiturating* [40] the enemy,
forgetting that everything is Vanity
and finally, willingly and *lowstoningly,* [41]
the man and the grub will be reduced to nothing.

Caterpillar of Love

When a caterpillar disappears it is a prelude
to getting lost between forms at every stage.
As a butterfly it will have manna from heaven
at the time of pollination with the illusion of sex.

He needs a real caterpillar to love.

He doesn't care if the flower is the channel
of food with his virtual female caterpillar.

He needs a real caterpillar to love.

The flower lives from pollen to seed,
the seed is the epilogue of the transition:
the dying seed generates a new life,
quivering at the vertex of being.
When does the grub live?
Through pollen or sex?

He needs a real caterpillar to love.

Wedding

The heart is ready to embark on a journey,
about to set sail on the high seas with his love.
In high spirits the groom heads to the altar
and from there out to sea
with sails billowing in the mistral
hoisting them on the nuptial bed of *zagara*.

The first roll of the waves blows
confetti and petals towards the altar:
among wafts of perfume
dancing ring-a-ring of roses
is accompanied by joyful singing.

On this day you can forget
politics, evil and malfeasance.

Round of Union

Festive singing fills the air,
as we celebrate through lyrics
pulsating with the elixir of life
in this magic moment of the dream.

An instant outburst of joy.

Bare flesh awaits
the light breath of air
from the diaphragm to the breast
longing to drink from the hell
of real and virtual love.

He drinks in warm kisses
lit up by reflections from the water,
giving in to instinct
but struck by thunder.
Acid rain may begin to fall,
but the acid of the world is power
that cancels finer feeling and goodwill.

A surreal war of love

Reality contaminates the rain with acid
damaging irrigation systems and
flooding the plains, while among grubs and men
war breaks out for a bit of straw.

The deluge ends with a clap of thunder.

A kite hovers overhead in a trance,
with shooting stars in a dance:
butterflies pirouette like rainbows,
birds drink in the moonlight,
and fishes blow plum-colored petals.

Love will flood over as a countervailing force
to the intrusions of the shadow of death,
but the threat of war will always hang over us.
Many are devoted to myth whereas
Ulysses, ruthless and treacherous,
betrays the code of ethics and loyalty.

Round dance

War and panic are in the air when caterpillars
join battle for female caterpillars:
it is not enough to beat your rivals
if the one you desire changes her mind.
Chance comes into play
as the law of the triangle takes over:
your love is all for the female caterpillar,
her love is all for the *ruga*. [18]

She is contended by the lovers,
ending with an exchange of intimacy
blossoming from an impulse
in that precise moment of authenticity.

And so the meeting of
like-minded souls goes on,
dancing to the sound of music,
the flame flickers out in a moment:
the charm of illusory magnetism.

Opposites attract

Illusion plays on the minds of caterpillars,
as they get up to their tricks,
like fairies dabbling in witchcraft,
placing their bets on the number ten:
this is gambling for caterpillars.

My love is for you and yours for him:
fate or chance do nothing to deal me
the winning numbers, favoring others.

My love is for you and yours for him:
the triangle does not work out well
and then destroys all hope.

In the void, loneliness binds us with a rope.

Upsets

Love exists only in a void
as emptiness bestows privilege
that unravels the reflected image
of the hidden mirror of essence.

Love has an impact on semblances
in a complex game of compensation
with fears arising from resistance,
leading to our absence.

Love is a convulsive affair,
but only by digesting pain
can you know the essence of your faith
leading to union with the present.

Tournament of two

The union of two is like a tournament,
though bouts of sleep may distract you,
diverting words from your thoughts
and from fusion with the firmament,
leading to the creation of new forms.

That which is new becomes a rite,
that is old in both politics and life.
We are saved from politics by reasoning,
and from life by moving forward:
in any case we end up running into the wall.

Everything is uncertain as it depends
on the outcome of the race between
competitors who are soon out of sight.
Recollections are powerful images
bringing emotions to life
in the shadows of the mind.

Rumbling states

Space imposes boundaries on views
that trespass into the abyss
while the caterpillar opens his arms
to the breath of wind on the breach
of the sublime neonatal state of worms.

Childhood moves on with the sound of stars
overflowing meteors of orange blossom
amid the loud noise of smell.

The powerful stench stops you in your tracks
as you move forward toward the landslide
though you find yourself in it up to your ankles.
You don't wish to step into the sinking sand
but can't hand over the reins to the wrong man,
as you reject the myth of the man on horseback,
the descendant of the perfidious Ulysses,
who set a dangerous precedent for men of straw.

Superfluous necessities

The need to pursue a life of love
is the price you pay
till you soften in the chainmail,
and the light shines in your eyes,
striking you with the ethics of mirrors
as the earthquake hits you
amid stamens and shadows in stalls.

You are convinced that you have to live,
but not as zombie caterpillars
inspired by visions,
so you will meet up with
a real, not virtual, female caterpillar,
and will know if your sorrow is soothed
only by colored screens.

Invisible exits

You approach her for inspiration
in spite of the *malamota* [(42)]
to tango in the swamp
where an *unstick-unstick*
will not spoil your game.
The water soaks you
with blue happiness,
entangling itself in vanity
whenever you draw any nearer.

There is no escape for the grub
crawling along the tree-trunk trough:
meeting her is a kind of game
but getting out of the swamp is a mirage,
as you think you are out but are still in,
a non-place on the outskirts or the city center,
with an exit hidden from sight
and out of the way.

Ghost traps

In our midst the dealers in antique ideas
weave spiders' webs of bridles
to draw into the quagmire
the purchasers of goods and vain ideas.

These comedians are fearless,
as they look for ways to make a profit,
reducing complex matters to a joke,
giving up unity for no reason,
assuming far-reaching powers,
and taking advantage of discontent.
Who knows whether democracy is in mourning?
The movement will not save the world, but
we need to be saved from false constructs.

The illusion of flying to the sun leads
towards the trap closing off the escape route
from dreams that transcend
sphinxes and puzzles,
simulacrums of fate.

Good omens

The caterpillar manages to guess
the origin of the ghost from the simulacrum
then moves on to eliminate all the omens.
Man is destined for defeat when he is
a defeatist who is half broken-down.

A shape looms ahead amid the omens,
like the remnants of a dream
that do not wipe out the memory
but show us the problems to be solved.

The riddle of immutable signals
brings forth fatuous words,
a convivium of vain and vacuous ideas,
sinking into the waters of the canal.

Fatuous borders

Sinking in the water
can be a normal experience
or a random episode.
Normally you learn to float,
but normality is the threshold
compatible with turmoil.

A *truguglio* [43] *abbiduglias* [44] it
in the belly-stench, [45] which huddle-paws [46]
rug-grease [47] of passions
unknown to trash-ignoring solitudes.
The sloth indulges them by taking pills
between *sgrulli* [48] of laughter with half-naked
female grubs, *sugliate* [49] with paillettes [50]
made red-hot by sabbatical [51] rhythms
in the disco of bullies,
where people *sbullas* [52] their thoughts
at the bedside, like zeroes with fallen-ears, [53]
thoughts made of awns, [54]
among the bistros on the frontier.

Residual strength

The frontier is found in smoke-filled bistros,
leaving no room for the thoughts of others.
The grub drives away such ideas and hides
in an underground tunnel,
on a path along the vertebrae of sleep,
emerging among signals sent to many,
but reaching few or not seen in time.
Blindness filters the signals that are evident
and signs of impotence that are unmistakable.

No way out is in sight,
and for the sake of dignity
it may be better to put an end to it
rather than living like a bandit.

Memory dust

Impotence heralds the end
for caterpillars, bullies, and others,
who are self-centered and against others,
no longer mindful of the journey they made
from the egg to the butterfly,
along the path of an introvert.

Nothing remains of caterpillars, nor of men,
as the breath of magic vanishes
in the rainbow of quicksand,
and emptiness fills
the recollection of pointless occasions.

All is lost in the distant echo, returning
love to those listening and diverting
the pain that changes perspectives to joy.
What then remains? Invectives of fragility
making their way down the road to hell.

Ultimate material

The road to hell is foretold in verses
that lie in the mud for a long time:
a heavy eternity of silence
that buries us in our absence.
Many martyrs lived their lives in vain,
only to be blown away in the dusty wind.

I was once a caterpillar.

I consist of hydrogen and carbon,
driving out songs and memories
of the hunt because at the end of the day
it is traces of nothing that remain.

At the end of the Cosmos

Memory is a chimera that deludes us
into thinking that we exist over time,
conveying the idea of life after death.
The Word says we should live in the present,
living according to the Word leads to torment,
and our reward starts from the moment.

Those who can, may live, whereas
those who have been struck down
by misfortune overshadowing their end
may not have the strength to welcome
the end and close the door,
as a result of pain or lack of support.

There are those who mouth words and songs
seeking enchantment (or vanity?)
in an attempt to play for extra time,
but the paper chase works against them
leading to oblivion and nothingness
from which nobody is exempt.

The landslide

Everything has gone with the landslide
and the earth turns into a desert
due to the strict laws governing nature
and the stupidity of the human race.

Everything has gone with the acid rain in the sky
as rivers breaking their banks cover the earth.
All living things may be wiped off
the face of the earth, but I feel far away.

Everything has gone as the wind blows,
but the smog has still not dispersed:
nothing at all remains in the air
but as a caterpillar, I feel far from the wind.

Everything has gone as fire spreads
across the face of the earth
collapsing matter into a black hole.
The caterpillar is a particle of lost energy,
but all will be devoured by a black hole.

Sailing away

The road ends here, where there is nothing,
and what was known is not known any more.
All that is knowable is to be found in the heart
leading to a new beginning.

There is no beginning of history,
as memory contains truth that hurts
and the end of the road is an enigma.
You need not be afraid to look into mystery
because life is like walking in a circle:
wherever you are, do the best you can.

1. NOTES

1.1. Editions

The first Italian edition was published in order to meet the deadline for a literary competition, leaving insufficient time to revise the manuscript carefully.

In the second edition about half the poems in the first edition were subject to substantial changes, while the other half underwent a minor revision. Moreover, it contained eight new poems at the beginning, after the first poem, which served, and still serves, as an introduction.

The third edition appeared when it was decided to release an e-book. During the revision of the published poems, some misprints were eliminated, and new compositions added. These examined the pressing issues relating to the Italian political and social situation over the last decade, resonating in the present and tending to obscure the wider horizon of the future. We need a collective effort and an individual commitment to the elaboration of critical thinking, which should be full of engaging and wide-ranging projects for social purposes aimed at *building community*. A reflection on these issues seemed urgent, even if the circulation is not on a large scale. It was decided not to wait any longer. As a result, the publication of the third edition was brought forward. Finally, it should be noted that the improvements made in some parts of the existing poems are limited in number and concern only some of the more impenetrable verses, that should perhaps have been deleted. Their inclusion may be a sign of weakness on the part of the author, who is particularly fond of them for psychological, ideological or stylistic reasons. Maybe these poems have been left only as a sign that the uniqueness of artistic expression does not exist. In fact, there are many definitions of the art of poetry, with subjective, diatopic, and diachronic variations, since arguably only existing elements give meaning to existence.

Finally, it should be noted that we have taken great pains to eliminate any typing and spelling errors in this edition but to err is human. As a result, the well-known incipit, "*ALLI BENIGNI LETTORI*" by the Turin typographer, Francesco Lorenzini, is still apposite. It is an express appeal to the readers' comprehension, included in the book of Achille Tatio Alessandrino, "*Dell'amore di Leucippe et di Clitophonte*" [About the love between Leucippe and Clitophonte], Venice, 1560. The original book, in the Italian of the seventeenth century, has been digitalized by Google and is accessible on the Internet:

"*In all human activities, it is almost necessary for mistakes to happen. However, the printing of books is the activity in which they occur more easily, in different ways, and for countless reasons. I cannot imagine any other activity, which is so subject to the risk of making errors. The task of correcting them appears to me like the story of Hercules and Hydra with the 50 heads: as soon as he cut off one head with his boldness and strength, two other heads appeared. Likewise, when an error is corrected with knowledge and diligence, several times we end up creating not two, but even three or four others. These are often of greater importance than the first. To tell how this can happen would require much longer discourse than is appropriate to this place. [...] I can truly assert that I could not ascertain that such mistakes did not occur in this book, notwithstanding all the diligent care I have applied to this work [...] Reader, if you find any such mistakes, which have occurred during the printing, according to your good and discreet judgement, you will be able to easily amend them. For courtesy of your soul, you will benignly forgive those errors, which through the fault of my weak intellect will truly be born of me. As a result, forgive me, as I have a nature capable of making mistakes."* (our translation)

This exoneration can also be applied to these poems, especially to the most tormented ones repeatedly modified over time, because simply deleting a poem from the collection is more drastic than making additions due to restructuring, projecting visions onto an uncertain horizon of stability of expression, where everything changes until it becomes myth. The myth itself must change to remain representative of the present, otherwise it dispels itself in the sun of immutability and dies in oblivion.

1.2. Lexical choices

The notes in this section are not explanatory in the technical sense of the term, but allusive, and refer to certain terms, often in italics in the collection, that are not to be found in dictionaries and may not be immediately clear to the reader. These notes reproduce those in the third Italian edition, even when the translation of the original terms has been simplified or in cases in which they were not used in the English edition.

The insights into these lexical items are set out below, also showing the number of the page where they appear in the poems. The possible explanations have been included, even if they are improbable and questionable, because a number of readers, some of them poets, have complained about the inclusion of certain dialect terms that are not familiar to everyone. In truth, this is not always the case, but this was sufficient to justify the partial indications given below. However, the reader is invited to approach these terms with a certain amount of imagination and sensitivity, according to the perception that arises from reading, which may vary over time. In this regard the Afterword is intended to clarify the fact that the unfamiliar terminology, used especially in three of the poems, resonates to some extent with the style of Fosco Maraini (*Gnòsi delle Fànfole*, Baldini Castoldi Dalai, Milan, 2007). These aspects concerned the Italian texts: in the English version they were reduced but not eliminated.

The dialect from which these terms are taken is that of the Abruzzo region, in particular Liscia, the remote mountain village in the province of Chieti where the author was born and bred.

Finally, it should be noted that "blend" is used in some cases to indicate compound terms consisting of syllables taken from more than one lexical item (Dardano Maurizio, Trifone Pietro, *Grammatica della lingua Italiana,*RCS Quotidiani/ Periodici S.p.A. under license Zanichelli, Bologna, 2007, p. 551; Luca Serianni, *Grammatica italiana*, second edition, UTET, Turin, 1991, p. 669).

1.3. Endnotes

Abbreviations used in the notes

fn = female noun
mn = male noun
pl = plural
pp = past/present participle

P. 39

[1] In Italian, 'of-verse' may also mean 'diverse' and *falli* can mean 'faults' and 'fouls'.

P. 41

[2] In Italian, *bozze*, consists of the first four letters of *bozzolo*, the Italian for 'cocoon'.

[3] The Italian term in dialect, *monnezza*, means 'garbage', 'rubbish' and 'trash'. It is to be found in the Italian dictionary.

P. 55

[4] The Treccani, the Italian Encyclopedia of Science, Letters, and Arts [*Enciclopedia Italiana di Scienze, Lettere ed Arti*], founded by Giovanni Treccani, is one of the great

encyclopedias rivaling the *Encyclopedia Britannica.*

P. 56

[5] In Italian, the term means both 'lie' and 'candle'.

P. 63

[6] *Union of opposites* was published in Nadia Cavalera (ed.), *Humafeminity – One hundred poet* for a linguistic-ethical innovation* [Umafeminità – Cento poet* per un'innovazione linguistico-etica]. Joker Editions, Novi Ligure (AL), 2014, 65.

P. 64

[7] *Uria*, the regional name of the south-easterly summer wind (*Scirocco*) that is generally fresh, in the author's region of Italy. It is mentioned in Battaglia S. (1961): *Great Dictionary of the Italian language* [Grande dizionario della lingua italiana], volumes 21 and two supplements, UTET, Turin.

[8] *Sticchio.* Pronounced: [*'stikkio*]. The meaning of this term varies from place to place. A common meaning is that of an object in the form of a parallelepiped or truncated pyramid (reference term, witness), which is used in a move. On top of this object the players place the stakes for each move: it was played in Liscia

(the remote mountain village where the author was born and bred) and was known as *pizzalle*. The game that uses flat stones has ancient origins. The discovery of the Neolithic site of Çatal Hüyük, a town in the Turkish province of Konya, in the ancient Lycia of Anatolia, 7000 years before Christ, suggests that even at that time it was in vogue to create stone spheres to play a game similar to bowls or bocce (see https://www.associazionegiochi antichi.it/giochi-tradizionali/famiglia-delle-piastre). *Pizzalle* was mainly played on the pavement by a minimum of two players. It consisted of a witness (*stêcchie*) on which coins, buttons, or other items were placed (stake). Each player was equipped with a stone slab (*pizzalle*) the size of one or two adult hands. A distance was determined from the witness from which to throw the stone slabs in turn towards the witness aimed at hitting it. If the witness was struck, the stake that was on it, or part of it, fell to the ground. The player took only the part of the stake closest to his *pizzalle*, with respect to the witness. The part of the stake closest to the witness remained in play and the players continued to play. The game ended when the stake was pocketed by one or more players. The next game began by placing a new stake.

p. 65

[9] *Mashed*, pp of the verb *mash* (in Italian *poltiglia*), a noun without a related verb in

Italian. This invented verb can indicate turning or reducing something (or someone) into mush or pulp. It can even indicate staying in the mash and similar cited terms.

p. 69

(10) *Fragaglia* was the original dialect term, which could be included in the Italian dictionary: it is synonymous with a medley, a chaotic assortment of items, a jumble.

(11) *Ammasticati*, pl pp, was the original term derived from the invented verb *ammasticare*, but it can derive from multiple combinations of Italian words that begin with 'am' (chosen according to taste) and chew, i.e. blends of am(...) + chew. It has been translated simply with 'to chew'.

(12) *Sbrígola*, the third person singular of the simple present tense (indicative) of an invented verb *sbrigolare*, meaning to emit, to finish off or to hurry. Pronounced: [*'sbri:gola*].

(13) *Sgruisce* was the original third person singular of the simple present tense (indicative) of the invented verb *sgruire*, which can mean to grunt, to crawl, and so on. The translation has been simplified with the verb 'to blow'.

(14) *Arruffanato*, pp, was the original term derived from the invented verb *arruffanare*, which can mean to get excited, to ruffle, to

upset, to destabilize. Ruffled comes closest in phonetic terms.

(15) *Arrampina*, the original simple present tense (indicative) of the invented verb *arrampinare*, that can stand for to climb, to claw, to clutch, to grapple with, and to taste.

(16) *Spriscia*, the original third person singular of the simple present tense (indicative) of the invented verb *sprisciare*, meaning to squeeze and deriving from a term in dialect. It can also stand for to squirt, to dart like a snake or *sbisciare* that is a Tuscan expression, or to spout, to spurt, to wriggle also in an erotic sense. The choice made here is to squeeze.

(17) *S'allupana* was the original third person singular of the simple present tense (indicative) of the invented verb *allupanarsi*, which can be intended as to get horny, to get excited (not necessarily with a sexual connotation), to ignite, to inflame and so on. The wolf is the animal involved in Italian terms.

(18) *Ruga*, fn, an Italian vernacular term, common in some regions, to indicate the caterpillar, but here it is allusive to other things, to that which can be exciting, as in the previous note, in particular, the female organs. Another meaning is 'wrinkle', which may be used in the same sense. Pronounced: [*'ruːga*].

(19) *Mopegno*, adverb/adjective, was the original dialect term, meaning 'stupid'.

(20) *Coccuta* was the original term in the Italian involving any of the meanings of the Italian term *cocca*, which may mean darling, pet, hen (in figurative language), favorite, with even some sexual allusions. Here, it has been translated as 'cockade'.

(21) *Strallazza*, the original third person singular of the simple present tense (indicative) of the invented verb *strallazzare*. Here, it is translated with the verb induce. However, *strallazzare* can be either a deformation of squawking (or fluttering or flapping its wings) with the same meaning or even a blend. Some examples of the first type of fusion: *stra*(godere) [to enjoy in an extraordinary way] + (intra)*llazzare* [to plot, to swindle]; *stra*(lciare) [to prune or to take away/ off/ out] + (intra)*llazzare* [idem]; *stra*(niare) [to alienate, to estrange] + (intra)*llazzare* [*idem*]. Some examples of a second type of fusion: *s*(polpare) [to take the flesh off] + (in)*trallazzare* [*idem*]; *s*(tanare) [to drive out] + (in)*trallazzare* [*idem*]; *s*(ucchiare) [to suck] + (in)*trallazzare* [*idem*]. In this situation, the possible combinations are numerous.

(22) *Sberlezzi*, pl mn, was the original term, which does not exist in Italian. However, the Italian *sberleffo* (mockery) is enough to indicate the context described in the text, but there is also something else, such as the blend of *sberleffo* and *lezzo* [stink, stench, filth] or *lazzo* [sour, tart, sharp or joke, jest], i.e. *sberl*(effo) + (l)*ezzo* or

sberle(ffo) [*slap, smack, bang, blow, chin, clout, cuff, deck, spank, wallop*] + (la)*zzo* [*idem*], but in this case it would sound better *sberlazzo* that alludes to *smerdazzo* involving shit and other similar nouns: crap, dung, poop, shite, and so on.

(23) *Ciamboni*, pl, stupid, simpleton; asshole, dickhead if you prefer the rhyming equivalent, but this is valid only in the Italian version. It derives from a term in dialect and its origin has never been clear to the author. The uncertainty between the big-dick as a possible English equivalent term and the original term was resolved in favor of the latter: *ciamboni*. Pronounced: [*tʃiam'bo:ni*].

(24) *Trombazzuti*, pl, was the original term, meaning pompous if used as a scornful, contemptuous terms. However, *trombazzuto* is more evocative because it adds the image of a great trumpet contained in the term. It may be more evocative if blended with another term, something like cock, dick or prick, i.e., *tromb*(one) [great trumpet] + (c)*azzuto* [badass and other coarse, vulgar terms]. The English blend is trumpdick: *trump*(et) + *dick*.

(25) *Sbidullati*, pl, was the original invented term, that does not exist in Italian and may be synonymous of idler/ loafer/ lounger/ sluggard/ bum, sloppy, sluggish or simply spineless, as translated here. It is the adaptation of a dialect

term (*svedellate*). For the truculent, it can also mean 'gutted', but it is a bit out of topic.

(26) *Arrufferie*, pl sf, was the translated term, which was close to robbery with stealth and violence. In fact, it has been translated grasp-robbery, although it is an ungainly expression.

(27) *Razzeccanti* was the original pp of the non-existent verb *razzeccare*, which can mean to put together, pick up or collect or gather or get together by arranging things close to something else. However, it should be noted that the subject is special also because the term 'castellan' sounds like 'Castilian'. In English, 'castellan' refers to the governor rather than the owner of the castle (the lord of the manor), while in Italian the lord of the manor is indicated with the same term. 'Castilian' and 'castellan' have a similar sound and are intended to allude to both meanings.

(28) *Ambòrie*, pl sf, is a blend of Italian words expressing multiple meanings. In fact, it is the result of a blend between love/ ambition/ ambiguity and *boria* [haughtiness, arrogance, ostentation]. It thus incorporates the meaning of the two or more terms: *am*(ore) [love] + *borie* [*idem*], or *amb*(izione) [ambition]/ *amb*(iguità) [ambiguity] + (b)*orie* [*idem*]. The English blend used here is lovrogance, i.e., *lov*(e) + (ar)*rogance*.

p. 70

[29] *Pointer*, noun, has various meanings, some of which are: (**1**) indicator, index, (**2**) hand of a clock, scale, and so on, (**3**) type of hunting dog, (**4**) suggestion indication (American), (**5**) cannon pointer (military). The intended meaning is in this military sense indicating one part of the torpedo, just as various other terms allude to parts of the torpedo.

p. 71

[30] *Ruffa*, noun, in addition to the meaning in the dictionary (crowd of people, taking or grabbing something) and evocations, there are other associations. One is to be found in *ruffello* (Tuscan expression), indicating ruffled or tangled hair or threads. Pronounced: [*'ruːffa*].

p. 79

[31] *Accatta* is the singular third person of the simple present tense (indicative) of the non-existent verb *accattare*, deriving from the French (*acheter*) meaning to buy. The term is adopted in some southern dialects and is to be found in some Italian dictionaries. See also the title of the Pasolini movie, *Accattone* (1961), meaning 'the beggarman'.

[32] *Sbidugliamento,* mn, was the original noun and can convey a range of images: from gutting or disemboweling to inactivity, from sloth to spoliation or plunder or pillage. It could be

considered to be the noun derived from *sbidullare*: see note (25). It is translated here with sluggutting: *slug* (ish) + (g) *utting*.

(33) S'*accozza*, the third person singular of the simple present tense (indicative) of the verb *accozzarsi*, but here it can imply becoming a mussel, approaching or attach yourself to something like a mussel. It is translated here with the non-existent verb in English: *to mussel*. The italicization in the text indicates this innovative use. The letter 's' at the end does not indicate the plural noun, but the third person singular of the simple present tense (indicative) of *to mussel*.

(34) *Merzelli*, pl mn, was the original term for sips or drips. It comes from the dialect, but is open to interpretation: drop, gulp, draught, and even morsel, which exists in the Italian and English dictionary with a sound similar to the original term. In fact, it is translated here with morsel.

(35) *Borboreggia*, the third person singular of the simple present tense (indicative) of the non-existent Italian verb *borboreggiare*, which can mean to grumble, rumble or mumble. More specifically it is an Italian blend of *borbo* (ttare)/ [to grumble, to mumble, to mutter] *borbo* (rigmo) [borborygm] + (rumo) *reggiare* [to rumble], but it is comparable in terms of vulgarity to farting. It is not a term intended to be used in polite company, but it may serve to

characterize the context. It is translated with (to) borborumble: *borbo* (rygm) + *rumble*.

(36) *Musicoregge*, fn, was the original term deriving from the combination of two terms, of which it takes on the meanings: music and farts, i.e., Italian blend of *music* (a) [music] + (sc) *oregge* [farts]; more refined is to combine it with reggae, for that particular musical genre. In English the term is musicfart: *music + fart*.

(37) *Berlocco* or brelocco, mn, a dialect noun derived from the French *breloque*, but existing as a loanword in Italian as *Brelocche, Brelocco, Berlocco*. It indicates the pendant that rests on the chest, hanging from a necklace or chain. In general, the term also refers to jewellery. It is typical of the author's dialect. Here the original French term was used.

(38) *Servazza*, third person singular of the simple present tense (indicative) of the non-existent Italian verb *servazzare*, which can have many meanings: to turn into servant if it is reflective, to gossip as a servant, to tittle-tattle, to act in such a way that the subject is tattling or saying tittle-tattle if it is not reflexive. It can also be used as a noun, as a pejorative term for a servant. This note is written with all due respect and love for those who perform this important and sometimes unjustly maligned function. Pronounced: [*ser'va:zza*].

(39) *Allinguando* was the original gerund of the non-existent Italian verb *allinguare*, which can mean to

lick, but also to lengthen the language toward the place which seems most pleasing to the agent or subject, with all the symbolic values related to this action. It was translated with the English blend (to) lentongue: *len* (gthen) + *tongue*.

(40) *Striturazzando*, the gerund of the non-existent Italian verb *striturazzare*, meaning to chop up in a derogatory and totally destructive manner. Suffice it here to use the English terms/verbs: crush, crumble, grind, mash, pulverize, rumple, smash, squeeze, shred. It was translated with an invented term (to) crutriturate: *cru* (sh/mble) + *triturate*.

(41) *Snocciolenti* was the original adjective or pp, spelling variant of the Italian term *snocciolare* (to stone). This variant was coined to better combine the new term with the saying *per duri nòccioli* [for hard nuts], which is an invented metaphor, also referring to hazelnuts. As a result, it is an Italian blend of *snocciol* (are) [to stone] + (l) *ento* [slow]. Here it is derived from the combination of the verb and the adjective, obtaining the verb to slow-stone, as in English the adjective generally precedes the noun. In everyday language, the expression is 'like it or not,' a short version. A longer version might be 'willingly and unwillingly'. By analogy, the term *slow-stoningly* was created.

p. 90

[42] *Malamota*, fn. Pronounced: [ˈmaːlaˈmoːta]. It is a blend consisting of *mala* – associated with the underworld, gangland, organized crime, gangsters – a Spanish term meaning *bad* and the same in the dialect of the author [due to the fact that the Spanish dominated southern Italy for centuries] and *mota* [mud, mire, sludge]. The nearest English term would be *bad-mud*.

p. 93

[43] *Truguglio*, mn, can oscillate between chip and concoction, between trough and turmoil, and associated meanings. Pronounced: [truˈguːljo]. Note that the exact sound corresponding to *gli* does not exist in English. In the International Phonetic Alphabet, it is represented by the symbol λ. As a result, it should be written as [truguλːo], but here the style for 'million' is used to approximate this phoneme.

[44] *Abbiduglia*, the original third person singular of the simple present tense (indicative) of the non-existent Italian verb *abbidugliare*, which can mean to deceive (to disappoint, to dupe, to entrap, and so on) by fooling or tricking the other party. Pronounced: [abbiˈduːlja].

[45] *Ventrume*, mn. The simplest meaning is a derogatory term for belly, but it can also be seen as a compound of belly and salami or costume or trash or fetidness (stench, rottenness). To

make it easier for the reader it has been translated as belly-stench.

(46) *Accalpita* is the original third person singular of the simple present tense (indicative) of the non-existent Italian verb *accalpitare*, which can simply stand for to paw, but with an additional syllable *acca* in front (in Italian). It can be used for huddling/ scuffling pawing. It is translated here as huddle-paw.

(47) *Stracciumi*, pl mn, is simply the pejorative of rag, not complying with grammatical rules, as an Italian blend of rag and sweets or bitumen or grease or other, i.e., *strac* (cio) [rag] + (dol) *ciume* [sweetmeat], *stracci* (o) [rag] + (bit) *ume/* [bitumen], (unt) *ume* [grease]. Other associations are possible. For the purposes of simplification, it is translated here as rag-grease.

(48) *Sgrulli*, mn pl or second person singular of the simple present tense (indicative) of the non-existent Italian verb *sgrullare*, which can refer to a slightly foolish (silly, stupid) person (noun) or action (verb). Pronounced: [*sg'ru:lli*].

(49) *Sugliate*, pp of the invented Italian verb *sugliare*, to dirty, to smear, to muddy. It was adopted in the dialect. It also derives from the French *souiller*, which, in turn, derives from the vulgar Latin *suculare*, which means to dirty. Some Italian dictionaries list the term *sugliardo*, meaning dirty, repulsive. It follows that the verb could be listed in the Italian dictionary, but also

in other dictionaries. Here it is left in the original to convey the original mysterious meaning. Pronounced: [*su'lja:te*].

(50) *Paillettes*, in the language of fashion, indicates what in Italian is called *lustrino*, and less commonly straw or small straw (Aldo Gabrielli, *Great Illustrated Dictionary of the Italian Language*, Mondadori, Milan, 1989). In this case there is a certain freedom of other visual associations. However, the term is sometimes used in English for 'sequins'.

(51) *Sabbatici*, pl adjective, is the original Italian term, with at least two meanings. First, it may refer to the general meaning of this word concerning the sabbat, not the sabbath (day). Note that Italian does not have an adjective like sabbatic or sabbatical. As a result, it was an invented term. Second, it may refer to (the rhythms of) Saturday night in the disco, and the free association (yours) with witches' and sorcerers' Sabbat. The corresponding English term *sabbaticals*, *sabbat* + (sabbat)*ical*, does not convey the full meaning of the original term because sabbatical exists without sabbat.

(52) *Sbulla*, third person singular of the simple present tense (indicative) of the non-existent Italian verb *sbullare*, meaning to unbolt. A possible blend is to bullbolt, *bull* (y) + (un) *bolt*, but perhaps the original term is better. As a result, the original term is used here. Pronounced: [*'sbu:lla*].

[53] *Morricce*, fn, derogatory term for an ear of wheat, which sounds like *spicastro* (spike, flower-spike), but this term has another meaning in Italian. The term comes from dialect and indicates ears of wheat left in the field by farmers during the harvest. The term indicates the object of gleaning. As a result, a compound of the two terms was used: fallen-ear(s).

[54] *Listre*, fn, is a dialect word denoting the awn or beard referring either a hair or bristle-like attachments of the spikes produced by many cereals. Hence, it is translated here as awn, a specialist term.

2. AFTERWORD

2.1. By way of presentation

The mysterious cycle of life is epitomized by the butterfly, who lives in the open air in its final stage of development. The early stages appear to be less appealing and, in a certain sense, a form of underground life, the price of becoming a butterfly. The caterpillar stage, limited as it is, excites the imagination due to the many associations. In fact, caterpillars are often considered to be repulsive, lowly, disgusting and ignominious. This stage may be seen as a life lived on the ground (perhaps for this reason, it is so often deprecated) and provides an interesting point of view: that of a powerless being, or an outcast. The purpose in this collection is to express in verse, or to sing the praises of this inferior being, with reflections in a major and a minor key, with the emotions and frustrations that can emerge from the larval stage, with the impulses arising from anger, with the disputes emerging from the devouring of books. As a result, the style is in a minor key and somewhat obsolete or, only by contrast, new and greater than the major key.

The title, *Life in B minor*, originates from these conditions. The B is the emblem of life lived in a minor key and also indicates the second promotion category in football competitions in Italy or the musical note or the cantata in a minor key, which in this case also has a conditional value and not just a musical one. The title therefore represents the main theme, but this vision is not unique and reflects only one aspect among the many present, as in a kaleidoscope. In a diachronic perspective, it can be added that it replaced the initial title, *Bacanetteratura urbana*, which was less immediate and more complex because it derived from the fusion of different terms and denoted both the content (the literature of bugs) and a negative value (garbage collection, which is not necessarily something negative), and the style that intended to hint at an intellectual and abstract approach. This blended term was, derived from the Italian: *ba*(co) [caterpillar] + *ca*(suale) [random] + *nette*(zza) [cleaning, which is referred to the 'municipal street cleaning and refuse collection' service] + (lette)*ratura* [literature]. At least in the first compositions there was an anti-*Anterem* spirit, that is, there were contrasting intentions to the style of the *Anterem* literary group. Over time and as the poems took shape, this turned into a more colloquial and relaxed tone. Due to this progression, the texts make the transition from allusion to contestation. Presumably, these are weak arguments because there are always many alternatives and the choices are only preferences. As a result, it makes no sense to examine other implications. In this edition, the cryptic and symbolic style, characterizing the imitative approach adopted for contrastive purposes, is partly diluted, especially in the explanatory notes, aimed at greater clarification than is usually to be found in poetry, for the purposes of unambiguous communication.

Refracting human meanings through the prism of another species is often to be found in literature because it allows greater freedom of expression, as the saying goes, from another point of view, which is always ours, but it belongs to a stranger in fiction. As a result, the language must be coherent and adequate to the bizarre situations while deploying more daring metaphors and unusual paths or more creative expressions. You can tear the curtain down but, in any case, the caterpillar has done so. You can say that humans are less than caterpillars. In any case, the caterpillar has already said it. A concept can be expressed clearly and explicitly, otherwise how would caterpillars be able to understand? You can mix unfamiliar and familiar words with totally invented ones that suggest meanings only with sounds or borrowed from an unfamiliar dialect conveying certain meanings. This is enough for the readers to fill in the rest with their own insights or imagination.

Much remains to be added, not by the author, but rather by the reader, who will hopefully manage to read the collection of poems all the way through to the end without ending up out of breath.

2.2. Lost in translation

Translation is a process transcending the original poetic text. In fact, especially in poetry, each line allows for many textual interpretations, as many as there are readers or translators, each allowing for a unique vision, starting from the original work. The translation process includes the phenomenon of domestication, i.e., modifying words and allusions, limiting polysemous expressions with multiple meanings, reducing anastrophic sentences, and making adaptations aimed at improving the readability of the source text by making it familiar to the reader in the target language. An author who translates the text himself without having an in-depth knowledge of the target language, as in this case, may produce a translation not of the same quality as the original. The author's room for manoeuver is therefore limited. Clearly, changes have been made in various parts of the translated version, though an effort has been made to remain faithful to the original.

Translation is a complex process, that cannot be examined in depth here. Rather, the aim of this note is to explain to the reader some of the choices made by the author. The guiding principle is that an effective poetic text should be faithful to the original, despite the losses resulting from translation.

It is evident that poetry is the result of a series of linguistic choices concerning the rhythmic structure, the selection and the collocation of words, in a sequence regulated by the principle of equivalence, that is, considering the strict semantic and phonetic nature of the text.

Rhyme is the most evident case of phonetic equivalence between the two versions of the poems, which is inevitably lost. In some cases, it is freely reconstructed with adaptations so that it no longer corresponds to the original text. Rhyme is related to certain rhetorical elements, including assonance, consonance, paronomasia, alliteration, imitative harmony, and onomatopoeia. Many of these elements have been lost or at times reconstructed on a different level. It was impossible for the author to do this unaided and as a result an English language editor was asked to revise the poems to improve syntax, rhythm, and readability. However, this editing encountered the same difficulties of translation and the editor modified the original translation by the author. The results are obviously marked by his poetic sensitivity and his aesthetic taste, as well as the need to make the text more accessible to an English reader. In some cases, the author does not recognize his own translation at all, but even when he was uncertain about certain formulations proposed by the editor, he had insufficient knowledge to insist on his own version. As a result, the expression 'translated by the author', originally intended to be on the title page, was considered to be unsuitable or incorrect in the end. However, the exchange of ideas between the author and the editor was a means to find the best possible adherence to the original and to respect the author's preferences. It turned out to be an interesting experience for both.

The semantic equivalences concern the figurative devices, such as simile, metaphor, metonymy, antithesis, and so on. Clearly there is no poetry without rhetorical devices. The translations are in many cases more readable than the original, even if the results are less effective, though at times they can be just as convincing.

In some cases, invented or acrostic terms are used in the original version in Italian, not easily identifiable or deriving from any particular dialect. It is not possible to reproduce them in any other language, so they have been translated to convey a particular meaning, as indicated in the notes.

Terms of this kind were present in some of the poems and have been translated into English or left in the original, but all have been explained in the notes, that are also to be found in the original version.

In conclusion, something may have been lost in the translation from the original, including the full meaning of a number of expressions, but at the same time something may have been gained, in terms of simplicity and immediacy, making the poems more readily accessible. Moreover, the original verses were reformulated without reproducing the metrical pattern. This may seem to be a loss, but it safeguards the original ideas and can even lead to more satisfying outcomes.

The English version is not intended to be a word-for-word translation of the Italian, or even a parallel text, but a new edition in its own right, since an extensive amount of reformulation was carried out primarily for stylistic purposes. In this connection I would like to extend my immense gratitude to my English language editor, William Bromwich, for his unfailing patience, his painstaking attention to stylistic matters, and his numerous cogent arguments that brought me round to his point of view.

Biographical Note

Michele Lalla was born in Liscia (Chieti) in the Abruzzo region in central Italy on 18 February 1952. He graduated in physics at the University of Rome in 1976 and since then has lived in Modena, teaching (social) statistics at the Marco Biagi Department of Economics at the University of Modena and Reggio Emilia. He has published books of poetry in dialect, as well as novels and essays in Italian.

The dialect poems were published in *Poesie in dialetto abruzzese: 1970-2020* [*Poems in the Abruzzi dialect: 1970-2020*] (Amazon, self-publishing, 2020), including three previous publications: *Storie vère o 'nventate* [*True or invented histories*] (Solfanelli, Chieti, 1983); *Scurciature de memorie* [*Short cuts of the memory*] (Campanotto Editore, Pasian di Prato, Udine, 2001); *Dê nche éune* [*Two through one*] (Campanotto Editore, 2012), which already contained a revision of the texts in *True or invented histories*.

The collections of poems in Italian are *L'Eco del Silenzio* [*The Echo of Silence*] (Lalli, Poggibonsi, 1984), *Il Vagito della Primavera* [*The Cry of Spring*] (Lalli, Poggibonsi, 1985), *Treninternet-viaggi* [*trainternetravels*] (Campanotto Editore, 2006), *Le cinque stagioni* [*The Five Seasons*] (3rd edition, Amazon, Lexington, KY, USA, 2018, pp. 1-310, with an e-book version and including the publications of 1984 and 1985), *Vita in B minore* [*Life in B minor*] (3rd edition, Amazon, San Bernardino, CA, USA, 2019, pp. 1-131, with an e-book version), *Giostra di haiku* [*Carousel of haikus*] (ilmiolibro.it, 2nd edition, 2015).

The prose compositions are: *La condanna* [*The sentence*] (in Premio Letterario – Racconti inediti, 2nd edition, anno 2006, Circolo culturale Archeosofia, Modena, 2007); *Trovare il senso: 70 storie zen occidentali* (3rd edition, ilmiolibro.it, 2015 – translated into English by the author and revised by William Bromwich, *Making Sense: Seventy Western Zen Stories*, Amazon, e-book 2015 & book 2016); *Andrò in America – 1. Il costo dell'orgoglio* [*I Will Go to America – 1. The Cost of Pride*] (3rd edition and e-book, ilmiolibro.it, 2015); *Partita con la vita* [*Match with life*] (in Andrea Piazza, *Il campo di pomodori e altri racconti* [*The tomato field and other tales*], Morellini Editore, Milan, 2014, pp. 109-131); *Il ragazzo con gli scarponi* [*The boy in the boots*] (in Cristina Pennavaja, *Tango argentino e altri racconti* [*Argentine tango and other tales*], Morellini Editore, 2015, pp. 45-84); *Profumo di magnolia* [*Magnolia scent*] (in *Racconti emiliani* [*Tales from Emilia*], no. 6, Consulta libri-e-progetti, ReggioEmilia, 2015, pp. 117-120); *Furto e carrello* [*Theft and cart*] (in *Racconti emiliani* [*Tales from Emilia*], no. 7, Consulta libri-e-progetti, Reggio Emilia, 2016, pp. 119-122); *La rinuncia di Eva* [*The renunciation of Eve*] (in *Racconti emiliani* [*Tales from Emilia*], no. 8, Consulta libri-e-progetti, Reggio Emilia, 2018, pp. 83-86).

Dialect poems published in: *Diverse LinguE* [*Diverse LanguagES*] (12: 155-161/ 1993, 15: 143-151/ 1996, 19/20: 125-134/ 1998 – all included in *Scurciature de memorie* [*Short cuts of the memory*]); *Tratti* [*Traits*] (Mobydick, Faenza 35: 10-13/1994). Italian poems appeared in: *Frontiera* [*Border*] (supplement to *Gli immediati dintorni* [*The immediate surroundings*], Bologna, 5: 38-39/1997); *Origini* [*Origins*] (La Scaletta, San Polo di Reggio Emilia, 39: 73-74/1999); *ilfilorosso* [*the-red-thread*] (51: 7/2011).

His literary writings include: "*Answers* to the Questionnaire for Poets in Dialect" (*Diverse LinguE*, 16: 19-28/1997), reviews and essays in *ilfilorosso* (**46**:51-53/2009, **49**:35-37/2010, **50**:48-51/2011, **52**:44-48/2012, **54**:53-56/2013, **55**:47-51/2013, **56**:40-43/2014, **57**:46-49/2014, **58**:46-51/2015, **59**:48-52/2015, **59**:55-59/2015, **60**:43-47/2016, **61**:36-4 1/2016, **63**:36-44/2017, **65**:50-51/2018, **66**:21-27/2019, **67**:43-46/2019).

Made in the USA
Monee, IL
16 May 2022

96529657R00079